The Incredible Saint Patrick

From Slave to Saint, a Life of Compassion and Courage

Jennifer S. Goins

This book is dedicated to my family and
especially my girls for whom I wrote it.

May all who read it be moved and inspired
by this special story of an incredible life!
Blessings to you!

Love,
Jennifer

A long time ago at the end of the 4th century AD, the great Roman Empire with its famous army legions, chariots and coliseums was in decline. In the western region of the crumbling empire lived a respected Roman family with a legacy of service to God. They had a son named Sucat. His Latin name was Patricius, meaning "noble". We know him today as Patrick!

Patrick grew up in Roman Britain near the sea shore. His parents, Calpurnius and Conchessa, loved God and taught him how to pray. Both his father and grandfather served in the local church. However, Patrick himself did not truly know God.

Despite the stability in his family, the world Patrick grew up in was dangerous. Various barbarian tribes were regularly attacking and invading the empire on the mainland. As a result the Roman army left the island of Britain to defend it.

Defenseless, Britain was vulnerable to attack, and when Irish raiders landed on the shores of Patrick's small village, they were unable to protect themselves. At the age of sixteen, Patrick was captured by these raiders and taken away to Ireland.

Once there, he was sold as a slave to a warrior chief who put him to work herding pigs and other livestock. For the next six years, Patrick was left to live out on the land with the animals. Cold and alone, he did not understand these strangers or their ways as he watched them worship the sun, moon, stars, elements and unknown spirits. In his isolation and sadness, Patrick turned to Jesus. He remembered the stories his family told him and how he was taught to pray.

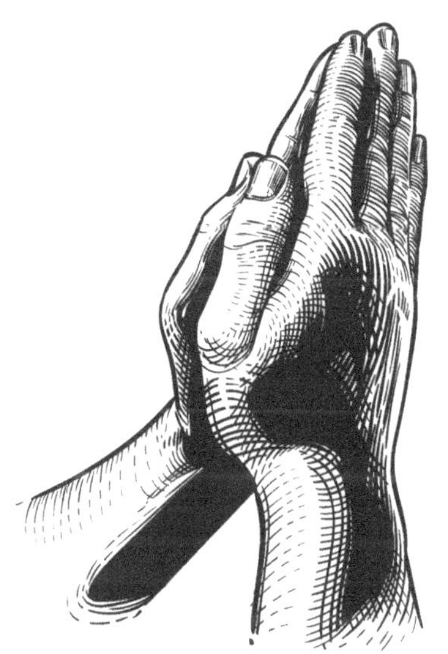

There on the hills of a foreign island, Patrick began praying to God. He prayed and prayed, often filling the entire day with prayer. Rain or shine, no matter the weather, he prayed, and as the days passed, God strengthened him and revived his soul. In fully submitting his life to Jesus, he found he was no longer alone. Through God's mercy and provision, Patrick was kept safe and grew strong.

Over time his relationship with Jesus blossomed. He even began hearing God responding within him, recognizing the voice of Holy Spirit! One day Holy Spirit gave Patrick word of a ship that would be his escape from slavery. So, he fled his master's land and traveled for days, hiding, running, guided only by Holy Spirit until he came to the seashore and found the foretold ship waiting.

Initially, Patrick was denied entry on the ship. So, he again prayed. Surprisingly, before his prayer ended, he was welcomed aboard and put in charge of some large Irish Wolfhounds who obeyed his every command at the astonishment of his shipmates! After learning that these seamen did not know God, Patrick took up the challenge of sharing Jesus with them.

During the trip a storm arose and blew the ship off coarse. Instead of landing safely in Britain, they arrived in France! The region they landed in was war torn and empty. With no food and supplies, the crew wandered for days suffering severe hunger and thirst. In a desperate moment, the captain challenged Patrick to pray to the God he had been preaching about! So, he did!

Suddenly, a herd of pigs appeared before their eyes. The miraculous provision supplied enough meat for all the crewmen and hounds to regain their strength. God continued to provide food, fire, and fair weather for the rest of their journey until they reached civilization. Patrick remained with the crew as their captive for two more months until the Holy Spirit again guided him to freedom, then to Britain and his family!

One night after being reunited with his family in Britain, Patrick dreamed of the Irish people desperately calling him back to Ireland. Their cries touched his heart so deeply, he abruptly woke up! Believing this to be his life's calling, he became determined to enter the ministry so he could return to Ireland and fulfill his destiny.

Years passed before Patrick's dream was fulfilled and he was allowed to return as a missionary to Ireland. It was a land of war, other gods, mysteries, and magic, which made his new mission risky and difficult.   Upon arrival, natives tried to drive Patrick and his fellow monks away, but eventually, he made peace with them and began to travel from kingdom to kingdom sharing the gospel through teachings and illustrations. Though his life was often in danger he persevered through the favor and power of God.

Regularly, he demonstrated courage
and supernatural power which
surpassed their magic. Once Patrick's
prayer over a snake infested
region miraculously repelled all
the snakes and drove them out to
sea! Time and again the kings,
chiefs, peasants, and druids of
Ireland saw a fearless man of
God willing to risk
it all to share God's
power and love with
them. They admired
Patrick and listened to him.
He challenged them, and
his boldness moved them to
faith.

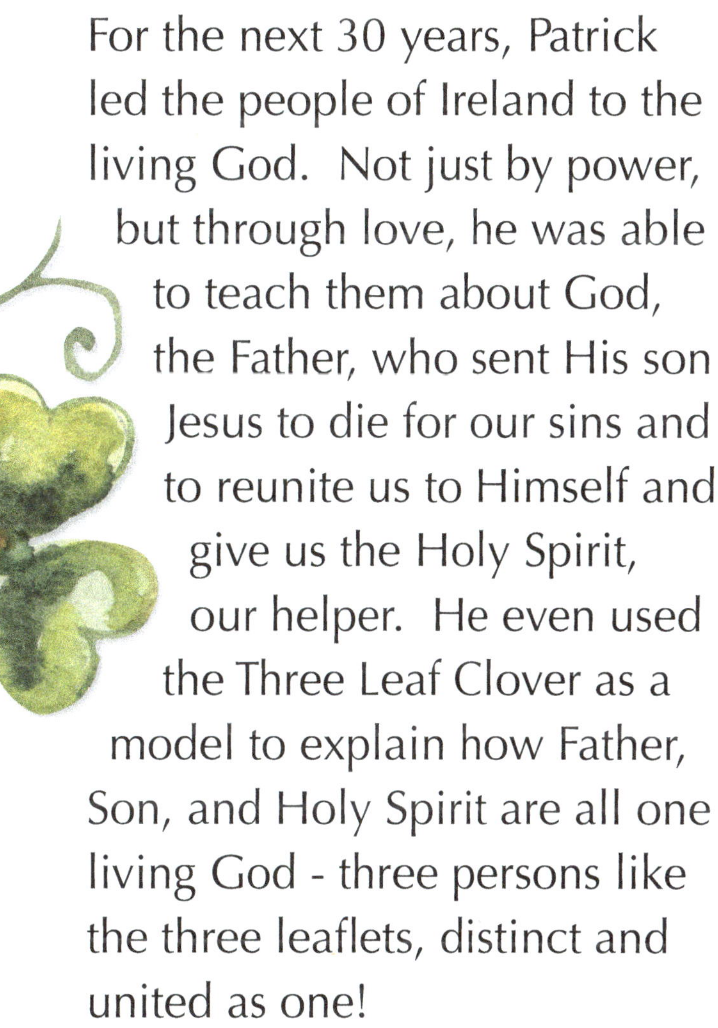

For the next 30 years, Patrick led the people of Ireland to the living God. Not just by power, but through love, he was able to teach them about God, the Father, who sent His son Jesus to die for our sins and to reunite us to Himself and give us the Holy Spirit, our helper. He even used the Three Leaf Clover as a model to explain how Father, Son, and Holy Spirit are all one living God - three persons like the three leaflets, distinct and united as one!

Ultimately, Patrick himself was the best model of Jesus' life and love as he, too, forgave his captors and embraced the people. During his mission, Patrick founded over 300 churches and baptized thousands of believers. His missionary legacy later led to Celtic Christians going forth from Ireland and re-evangelizing Western Europe. Patrick died around 461AD, having fulfilled his calling, giving all the glory to God! Two centuries later, he was awarded the honor of sainthood.

Much of what we know about him comes from Patrick's own written confession. His life was marked by trials, faith, power, and love. He opposed slavery, encouraged others, taught the masses and risked his life in order to bring his enemies to the same faith that saved him. Patrick knew the grace, love, and power of God, and it is available to you, too!

Image Credits

Ancient Rome. ID 103594403 © Netsign33 | Dreamstime.com

Roman Boy Vintage Illustration. ID 163317082 © Patrick Guenette | Dreamstime.com

Strong Viking on Ship. Adapted to Illustration. ID 71405386 © Khosrork | Dreamstime.com

Viking Ships. ID 46066059 © Macrolink | Dreamstime.com

Set Viking. ID 125867008 © Potysiev Denis | Dreamstime.com

Irish Landscape. ID 97743679 © Buccaneer | Dreamstime.com

Praying Hands. Adapted to Black & White. ID 86067036 © Microvone | Dreamstime.com

Watercolor Pentecost. ID 189236911 © Svetlana Vorotniak | Dreamstime.com

Viking Ship. ID 8119689 © Makarova Olga | Dreamstime.com

Temple Ruins. Adapted to Illustration. ID 41436814 © Melkor3d | Dreamstime.com

Herd of Pigs on Pasture. Adapted to Illustration. ID 170557686 © Sabine Seiter | Dreamstime.com

Saint Patrick Blesses the Irish. ID 163223625 © Patrick Guenette | Dreamstime.com

Man Naps. Adapted. ID 231067735 © Vika12345 | Dreamstime.com

Saint Patrick Expelling Snakes. ID 139703431 © Anton Tokarev | Dreamstime.com

Snakes Watercolor. Adapted. ID 173601270 © Nolimolly2 | Dreamstime.com

Watercolor Clover. ID 67045355 © Tetiana Kozachok | Dreamstime.com

Rock of Cashel. Saint Patrick's Rock. ID 163050648 © Patrick Guenette | Dreamstime.com

Stone Cross. ID 247755 © Paul Moore | Dreamstime.com

Three Leaf Clover. Adapted to Watercolor. ID 30548764 © Helioshammer | Dreamstime.com

Rivière. A Legend of Saint Patrick. Adapted to Drawing. ID 22379533861 © Public Domain Image. Art Gallery ErgsArt - by ErgSap | Flickr.com

A Legend of Saint Patrick. Briton Riviere. Adapted to Drawing.© Public Domain Image| yigruzeltil | Wikiart.org

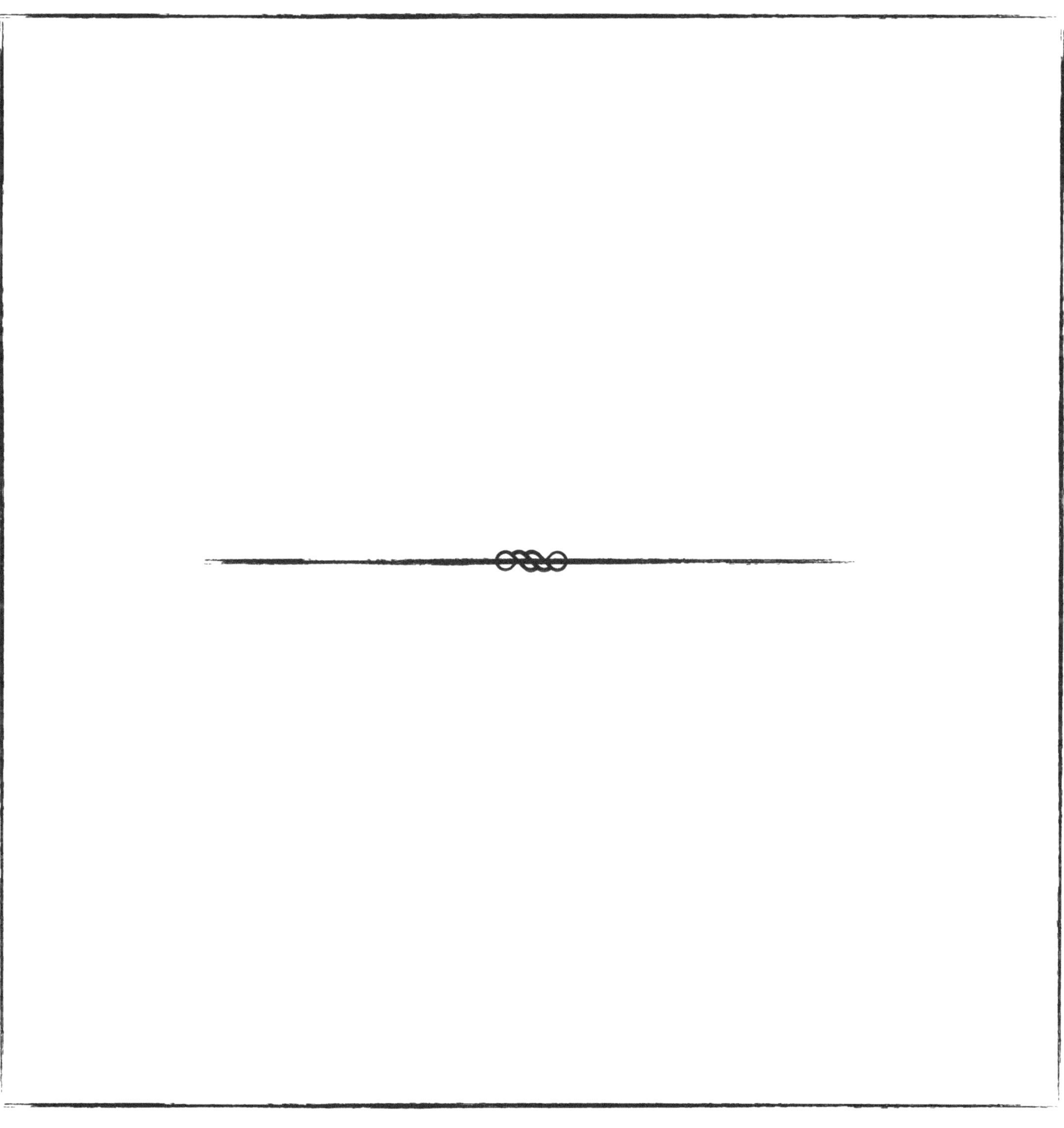